LILAC LIBRARY

POETRY TO EXTEND, EXPLORE AND EVOLVE

VANSHIKA MUKHERJEE

INDIA • SINGAPORE • MALAYSIA

ISBN 979-8-88733-683-1

CONTENTS

SECTION 1:

Intro: Begin

To mark the start of my first book, 'Intro: Begin' consists of a few poems I wrote when I had just started writing poetry.

This section highlights the fact that every beginning counts, no matter how small or imperfect you think it is.

1

HOW IT ALL BEGAN

It's 2020,
And the world has paused.

Silences are emptier than they used to be,
The uncertainty has become too loud.

To find a balance between the two,
I started to write.

People call it poetry,
I call it an attempt to hush the screams of doubt.

An effort to keep me sane when the world we once knew,
Exists no more.

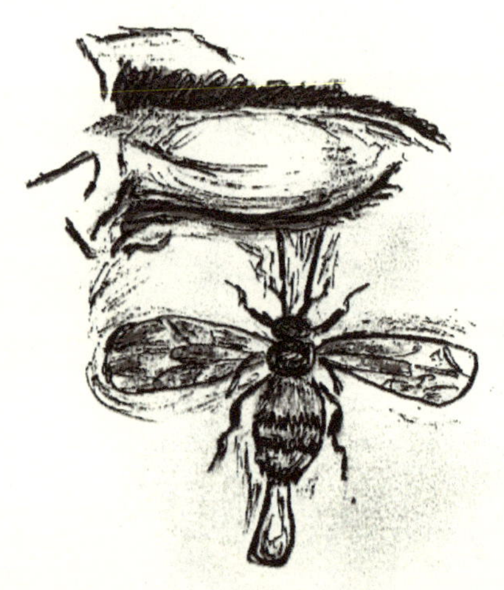

2

BEAUTY OF TEARDROPS

Teardrops on my face,

Fresh as a raindrop on a leaf,

Remind me of the colours of nature.

Sometimes, they shine so bright under the daylight,

While at other times, hide beneath the layer of dust.

My tears are just as beautiful,

Just as sweet as honey.

Sometimes, they come from sadness and other times, from happiness,

But every time, they're just as beautiful,

As a raindrop on a leaf.

3

CHILDHOOD NOSTALGIA

We used to run around with smiles on our faces,
Not a hint of woe on our minds,
The whole world appeared so cheerful.

Every person was our friend,
Dreams sprouted in our minds,
Like flowers in bloom.

Nothing was as gloomy,
As the late winter's moon.

Wish I could go down memory lane,
Visit those places again.

The daisies that bloomed in my heart back when I was an infant,
Haven't withered yet, so the child in me is still present,
But this childhood nostalgia will never see an end.

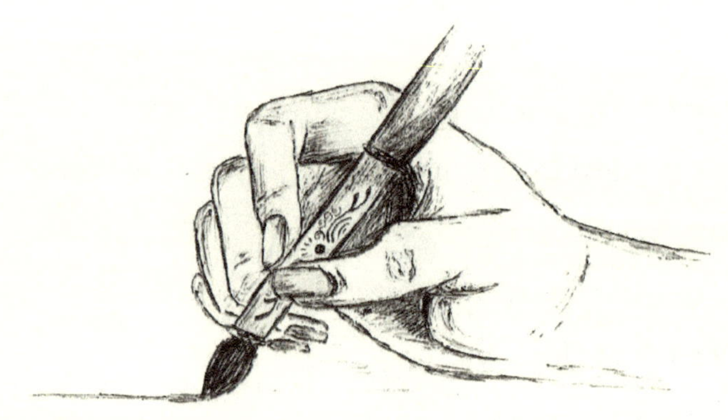

4

DÉJÀ VU

Vibrant splashes of orange and pink across the sky,
Resemble a painting on a canvas,
That I painted in my dream.

Is this a déjà vu,
Or the waking dream
My heart longed for?

Name it whatever you want,
But to see this unfold before me,
Is a wish fulfilment for my heart.

Someday, I'll pick up my brush,
And make a stroke or two,
To capture this déjà vu,
And wish my dream adieu.

5

HUES OF TIME

The world of the present,
Seems nothing like the world of the past.

This spilt second in the expansive time,
Is filled with monochrome coldness,
But highlights the shades of time in this world's prowess.

What might seem dull at the moment,
Will light up with a tiny spark,
Spreading the light of hope and joy,
To the masses who've had hundreds of sleepless nights.
Sinking low with the weight of their aching souls,
Their gazing eyes will fill up with colours again,
A day will come with an end to all this pain.

The winter might seem harsh at this moment,
But no season is eternal,

The night is always the darkest,
Before the first light of dawn.

Just like that,
Our cold and dark winter will come to an end,
The flowers of spring will blossom once again.

Just hold on a little longer,
Our spring day is just around the corner.

SECTION 2:

Earthly/Cosmic Magic

I've always been an admirer of nature and its beauty, resulting in a number of poems written about the various elements of nature. Similarly, the universe beyond our earth has been my muse for a couple of poems.

So, this section holds within itself the beauty of our universe through my eyes.

1

PETRICHOR

Pitter-patter on my windowsill,
Droplets announce the coming of a thunderstorm,
One that sends the meadow into an unrest.

Bushes, trees, all the greenery shakes frantically,
Under the spell of the wind,
But when the raindrops multiply in number,
Everything slows down.

All the living beings,
Big and small, short and tall,
Come together to see the wonder,
The wonder of the blessed rain.

Rain quenches the thirst of many,
Giving a melody for our hearts to cherish,
A melody to restore peace, and make the unrest vanish.

2

MOONSHINE BLUES

The moon is so lucky,
It gets to nap around clouds so soft,
Rest its head,
And still stay aloft.

Fly in the jet black sky,
And gift the children on earth,
Dreams of things so radiant.

I wish I could snap my fingers,
And give the gift of light,
To our lovely planetoid,
Because it fulfils the dreams of millions,
But still lives in solitude,
In the unending black sky.

It stays hanging in the air,

For hours at end,

We murmur soft praises when it changes colours and sizes,

But never realize,

That those might get lost in space,

The empty black space,

Where the moon lives alone, so alone.

But then I cognize,

Aren't we, the people,

The same as the moon?

We talk to each other, not letting our guards down,

Try our best to shine for our kinfolk,

While hiding our deepest fears,

And never letting them see our dark side.

Do you see how similar you are,

To the white pumpkin in the sky?

The one that you always look up to,

But never comprehend.

You are the moon of your life,
The one who shines bright,
Surrounded by people,
Yet lone, so lone.

3

HEAVENLY LOVE

Under the silvery moonlight,
The stars fall from the sky,
Like raindrops under sunshine,
Covering me like a blanket,
With the warmth I always longed for.

Creatures of the dark sing harmonies,
Mesmerized by the night sky,
To me, those are the lullabies,
That send me love from all celestial bodies above.

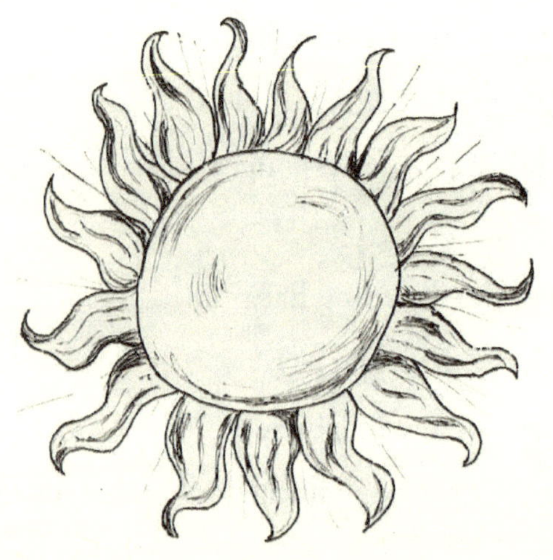

4

SUN, MY DEAREST

Dancing under the golden rays,
I smile from my heart and soul.

I look up at the sky every day,
And wish the sun loved me more.

I admire how generous it is,
Embracing us with its light,
Spreading a warmth that lasts through the night.

Till the day it shines,
Let me lay under the sun.

A day may come when we become friends,
And it gifts me a heart of gold.

It may take a thousand years,
Or maybe just a few,
But till then,
This tale shall continue on its own.

For now, we are young,
Both, me and the sun.

5

DEAR MOTHER EARTH

The soft mist that we wake up to,
After a rainy night,
Lush green meadows,
Sparkling in green under the sunlight.

The sound of water,
Flowing in a shallow stream,
All these little gifts of nature,
Far too pure to be seen by our naked eyes.

But such an honest display of earthly innocence,
Is a symbol of the motherly tenderness of the Earth.

Why not preserve this untainted being forevermore,
Instead of unloading all your toxic trash on her?

Why not gift back the present we were all born with,

Why not let the Earth breath again,

Why not let her thrive?

6

ARDENT LOVER OF SEASONS

With every new year,
The winter gets fiercer,
But it teaches us how to protect ourselves.

Then comes spring, knocking on our windows,
With its sweet smile, accompanied by a scent of newness,
Along with the fragility of flowers and a touch of the golden sunlight.

A time comes when this sunlight becomes a bit too harsh,
That's when you know summer has come around
With its unbearable heat,
A season for you to enjoy ice cream as a treat.

Monsoon will be short and sweet,
Bearing gifts of the wind and water,
Filling us with positive energies.

Next comes autumn,

A gentle reminder,

That it is important to discard what's needless,

No matter how attached you are,

Attachments are only healthy,

Until they enhance your beauty, not when they make it dwindle.

Winter comes back again with its open arms,

Brutal, yet comforting,

Disclosing the harsh realities with its chilly winds,

To make the burning ache subside.

These seasons teach me their simple lessons,

Every year in a loop,

But each time around,

The lessons become more enriched with life.

I empty my heart when each year starts,

Just to fill it with the gifts of the seasons,

New ones every year,

With a good deal of their magic stored inside.

I am an ardent lover of seasons,
They make me admire the change,
That I used to fear otherwise.

7

MY BELOVED SKY

I still remember,
The day I fell in love with the sky,
When the clouds held the sun in their honeyed arms,
Just before it said goodbye.

I watch the sky every day,
It changes colour like a chameleon,
Separate hues for every time of the day.

As the sky grows darker,
I cherish the twinkling stars,
And dive into the milkiness of the moon.

I wait for the sun to rise again,
So I can once again,
See the sky play with colours.

SECTION 3:

My time

'My time', as the name suggests, is the segment where you'll get a glimpse into who I am as a person.

All of these poems are very close to my heart as they are pieces that I came up with at various junctures of my life. Mostly, the poems included here have been written at different stages, as a strategy to reflect on how age brought changes to my personality/identity. At times, it might be difficult to understand what I truly mean, but that is the beauty of it all. There is a bit of mystery hidden between every word, along every line.

1

HER AND I

A girl of years twelve and a half,
With endless dreams and a river of puerile thoughts,
In the deepest corner of her heart,
There lay a garden full of butterflies and moths.

One that was inexplicably mesmerizing,
She saw it grow every minute of the day,
Bloom into a mixture of eternal beauty,
With flowers and mosses, herbs and grasses.

She wanted to spread her wings,
And fly in the open sky.

With the mini garden she grew,
She wanted to make the world her own,
A big garden, where she could frolic and roam.

Then, one day, came a ferocious storm,
Robbed her of her beauty and left nothing,
Nothing for her to cherish,
Just a dirty, unkempt lawn.

The girl you read about in the lines above,
Is no one but me,
A girl who lost everything she owned,
All dreams unfulfilled, unknown.

2

17

Tender hands and silken hair,
Smiles as sweet as honey,
Eyes that never tell a lie,
This was me as a child.

My childhood, a tale I remember,
So fresh, as if it were yesterday,
When I was a child.

A little has changed,
I stand a few feet taller,
Maybe, I am a little wiser.

But at heart I am still a child of nine,
Ready to take over the world,
With the magic I hold inside.

Now, I will make use of the ink of time,

Write a new story,

In the book of my journey,

On this road of life.

Imbibe the simplicity of blue skies,

Soak in the freshness of forests after the rain.

Step into adulthood,

With the old me,

That grew into a pretty girl of seventeen,

Ready to colour the world with new hues and tones infinite.

3

PHOSPHENES

Faeries and flowers,
Magic and superpowers,
My pretty little mind,
Made an abode of memories.

A little shabby place,
With colours and shimmering glaze,
I visit that place once in a blue moon,
To remind me of my roots.

Every sight I see,
Is a reminiscent of my childhood,
A golden memory,
That lives forever, in the little shabby place,
That my pretty little mind made.

The place puts together,
Every piece of me,
Like a beautiful puzzle,
With not one missing piece.

Even when I grow old,
I will not let the place out of my hold,
It carries my essence everywhere,
One that sums up my spirit.

Even today,
As I step into a new chapter of life,
I took a trip back to that little shabby place,
To remind me of who I am.

To rejuvenate my pretty little mind,
And make this new period of life,
Embellished with smiles and shine.

4

FEARLESS

The fire within,
Swallows me whole into its flames.

Tears that wet my cheek a while back,
Have become my strength today.

The hourglass,
Which reminded me of the time running by,
Has become the reason I can fight.

This fire that has been burning all along,
Felt too hard to smother.

But now, I have found me,
And the fire doesn't bother me anymore.

I can fly high in the sky,
With fire burning my wings,
Because I know, I won't crash on the ground.

A day shall come,
When the fire blows out,
And the ashes,
Shall be the reminder,
That even if flames surround,
I am a warrior, newly found.

5

A POET'S WISH

Letters that were never written,
Words that I never spoke,
Fill a void so deep in my heart,
It doesn't feel empty anymore.

I still feel them in my bones,
When the words try to tickle my spine,
Making me utter a word or two,
Letting my magic out,
In this world so colossal.

Wish that one day,
I find a way,
To let out all the suppressed emotions,
That reside in my mind,
In all forms imaginable.

Wish I could give away a piece of my heart,
To make the world experience,
The fairy-tale that I wrote,
And the hundreds of stories,
That remain untold.

Wish I could pen my thoughts,
Make them flow into an endless river,
For everyone to see and discover.

A world I built in my head,
So marvellous, it looks like a pretty lie,
I wish everyone could see,
I wish.

6

19

My last year living the 'teenage dream',
But maybe the first.

When I look back,
I only see a scared little girl,
Trying to make sense of the world.

Too young to make her own decisions,
Or to 'romanticize' her life.

Today, when I've lived half of my time
As a 19-year-old,
I'm finally beginning to understand,
How to live while I'm young,
Because I won't be this young ever again.

Nevertheless, who am I

To ask for a rewind?

Maybe, this is what youth actually is,

The realization that you have to make the most of your life,

Right now, in this moment.

A realization, that often hits a little late.

7

FUEL FOR MY MIND

Every once in a while,

I surrender myself to the saddening thoughts,

That often cross the streets of my mind.

They remind me of my worries, which I try to bury deep inside,

Sometimes, that is my reason to pick up my pen and write,

About things that prompt me to wonder,

Wonder about anything and everything, all at once.

Discover a way to triumph over my demons,

By using my words as an armour,

And my curious mind as a sword.

With each poem that I pour out,

A new worry is given a voice,

It's just so liberating to see them turn one by one,

From a thorny rose to a sunflower so warm.

There's something new to worry about on a daily basis,
That's a relief in disguise,
Since my pen will never run out of ink,
And my mind will remain immortally poetic.

SECTION 4:

Once upon a feeling

As a teenager, it is tough to figure out the world with the whole mess of emotions that are omnipresent in my mind.

The aim of this section is to take you on a journey, and view the thoughts that prevailed in my mind as I experienced a variety of feelings. I often found myself resorting to poetry to seek validation, and pour out my true emotions in order to provide some stability to my restless mind.

1

YOUTH IS YOURS

Leave the past where it belongs,
You belong right here,
In the present.

The past could hurt you in a million ways,
Or make you bloom in happiness,
But that bloom won't be as fruitful,
It's just a work of fantasy,
Written by your mind.

Your mind is a good liar,
Don't let it feed you it's pretty lies,
It might look very appealing,
To see your past dreams come to life.

But trust me,
Living in the past hurts,

Because it makes your present,
Crumble into nothingness,
And the future starts looking like a distant dream.

Here and now might be cruel,
But it's not forever,
For now, you are young,
The present is yours,
And so is the future.

But youth isn't forever either,
It won't come back to you,
No matter how much you whine.

Let time work its magic,
And someday,
You'll reach where you are meant to be.

2

CUE THE NOSTALGIA

The classroom I visited every day,
Is still so fresh in my head,
All the hustle and bustle of the classes,
Creaking furniture, whispering classmates,
Lectures of the teachers, ticking of the clock,
Tick-tock, tick-tock,
It flew by so quickly.

My time at what I believed,
Was my second home, my school.

What hurt me the most,
Is that I never got closure,
To all my years in school,
It started with a jolly ride,
And ended over a zoom call.

What has life come to?

14 years of my life came to an end,

With the click of an 'end meeting' button.

But I have no choice,

I'll have to pick up the pieces,

And step into a new phase of life.

But I do have something to say,

To the countless days I spent at school,

"You are my hardest goodbye."

3

MYSTERY OF THE WORLD

What are we,
If not an empty vessel,
With a bunch of emotions poured inside.

What is life,
If not an overrated period of time.

All of us get 24 hours, every day,
Yet we experience them so differently.

7 billion stories,
Trapped between the endless sky,
and the earth that dies, ever so steadily,
Giving into the cruelty,
Of the vicious humankind.

The tragedy of it all,
Is that everything we have is now,

Because we're crushing our tomorrow,
Under the weight of a past,
That was never truly ours.

The reality is that our universe is nothing but a vibrant cosmos,
Painted with every colour,
All at once.

Yet we continue to thrive,
In this flamboyant mess,
Because chaos is all we've ever known,
Peace and quiet, a fantasy unknown.

4

HAPPINESS

Happiness is a fairy-tale,
That I have always yearned,
The one feeling I couldn't help but crave.

I chased happiness in every possible scenario,
Blinding myself to the fact that in reality,
Happiness is just a part of our imagination,
A dream we wish was true,
An emotion far too exaggerated.

At the end of the day,
Happiness has been wronged by all of humankind,
Because even when we're truly happy,
We're never really satisfied.

This is why I've decided,
I don't want happiness,

I don't want to run after something
That is a mirage,
Constructed by people
Who enjoy it when others suffer,
Running laps in the same loop, a million times.

It took me a lot of time,
But I've finally come to realize,
That happiness is nothing,
But a metaphor for beautiful lies,
A bandage forced upon
Open wounds that never get to heal.

5

FOREVER IS A LIE

As I open my eyes,
I see the overcast skies,
Reaching out for you,
With my unfurled arms.

The ringing in my head,
Are the muffled alarms,
Telling me that our time is over,
Because forever was never a thing.

Flying with the power of our memories,
Suddenly, I fall to the ground,
With pain gushing through my veins,
You in my heart, the only thing that remains.

6

WHAT A SONG MAKES ME FEEL

Every time I plug in my earphones
To listen to a new song,
In my mind,
I'm fully ready to get transported to a different land,
Where the singer recites a tale,
Close to their heart,
Not too far from reality,
Yet too ethereal to be true.

I wait around for every lyric,
Closely examining every drift in emotion,
Only for a line to astound my mind,
And put me in a state of awe.

Fill me with awareness
Of a feeling, I never knew I felt before.

Gifting me a new perspective to hold on to,
A piece of the artist's heart,
Safe and sound in mine.

7

IF TODAY WAS ALL I HAD…

Once I come back home,
From a long day outside,
And the contented tiredness begins to sink in,
I drown myself in a river of thoughts.

The most recurrent one is always,
'Would the universe give me a sign?
If today was all I had,
And tomorrow was a faraway destination,
I was never meant to reach?'

SECTION 5:

Trivial treasures

I've always been a keen observer, keeping an eye on everything that attracts my attention. I often find myself taking notes of little things I encounter so that I can later put them out on a piece of paper, and truly enjoy the little gifts of life.

This section encapsulates a variety of themes, all mixed into one. But the aim remains to treasure trivial encounters, be it in the form of things, realizations, distinctive phenomenon, and everything in between.

1

LITTLE DISCOVERIES

Flipping through the pages of my favourite book,
I sit by the double-glazed window,
Bathing in the orange rays of the setting sun.

I skim through every line,
Re-reading the story,
I already know like the back of my hand.

Each time I return to this book,
I swear it becomes thicker,
And between every two chapters,
The wordless spaces recite a new line.

Something straight from the author's heart,
That never made the cut,
But still remained on the pages of the book,
A remnant of all the unfinished plots.

There is something so tender,
About drowning yourself in the scent of books,
And discovering something new with every read,
Yet leaving behind a little more to find every single time.

2

HEART: AN ENCHANTER

A heart that beats,
Has a soul that grows,
Fights battles on its own,
Makes its strengths known.

The delicateness of the heart,
Is an unfathomable art.

A heart holds power, so gentle,
Yet so wily,
It could weave you into a web of love,
That you can never fall out of.

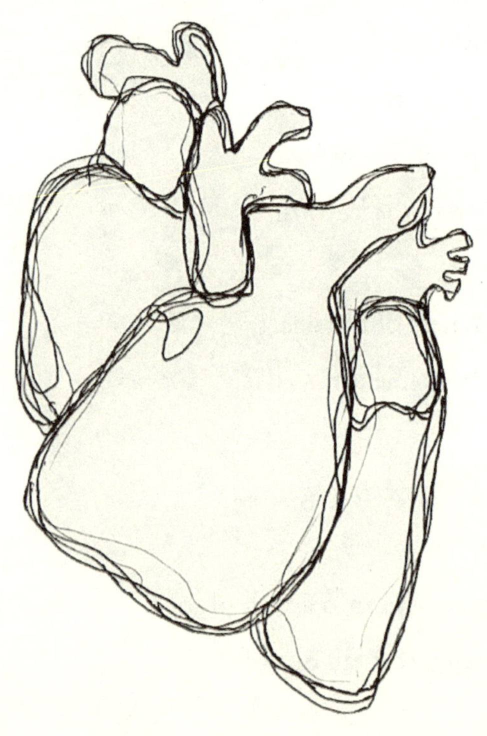

It breaks when people leave our side,
But still beats, like a broken record,
As a reminder that you have yourself,
Today, tomorrow, and forever,
Even when they say, forever is an illusion.

3

CARDIGAN

I found an old cardigan,
That feels like an old friend,
Who's engulfed me in their warm arms,
And offered me a trip down memory lane.

It held me close in dark times,
With unwavering tenderness,
Got splashed with paints from my palette,
But remained mellow on my skin.

So many car rides and footprints,
And unexplained silences,
I've spent with it draped around me.

All these years,
It was hiding in my wardrobe,
So, I could find it one day and say,
"I'm glad you always stayed."

4

A TALE OF TWO LOVERS

The minute and hour hands of a clock,
Only meet every once in a while.

They never get more than a minute together,
Still, never stop to complain.

They keep going on and on,
Doing their job without a halt.

I feel bad sometimes,
To see these two lovers,
Stuck in the cycle of time.

5

SIMPLE REALIZATIONS

Cycling everyday has become a hobby choice,
A liberating experience just to exist.

The wind combs my hair haphazardly,
And the music of the surroundings serenades me.

I realize as I pedal ahead,
How less we live,
And how much we merely survive,
In the hustle of these fast times.

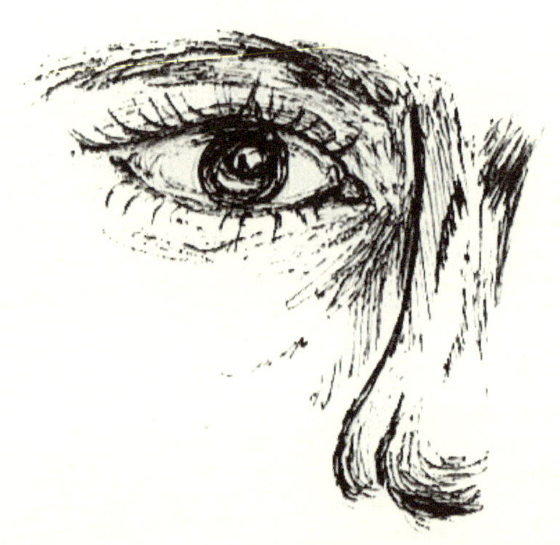

6

HISTORY IN YOUR EYES

Possibilities along the blank spaces,
As endless as one can be,
They reveal a thousand secrets,
Without disclosing any.

A silent utterance of words,
That is simply non-existent to many,
What a world it would be,
If we start paying attention to the spaces,
Spaces that have no clear meaning.

Just imagine,
How it would be,
If we all tried to fill in the spaces,
With words we never said,
And rewrite history,
With the moments we choose to live.

Zero plans, zero calculations,
Just a reimagination of the world,
Along the empty spaces,
That enclose the hidden history.

Open your eyes to the unseen reality,
To the stories hidden from all eyes,
Except for your bright and colourful eyes.

7

POETRY

Poetry,
What a fancy word!
Something that the world admires,
But only a few understand.

What is poetry?
Poetry is life,
Life from the perspective of a living soul.

It can take any shape or form,
It can make you cry or jump in joy.

Poetry is a world of the unknown,
No one really knows what it means,
But we all know it exists,
Maybe, that is all poetry is.

A proof that we all exist,

A symbol of life,

But what really is poetry?

I guess, we'll never know.

8

HOW TO (UN)LOVE

People lose touch and disconnect,
It's merely a progression in dynamic,
Nothing more, nothing less.

Hatred is not the only motive,
When your efforts are not reciprocated,
Some adventures just aren't worthwhile.

The moment you sense a withdrawal from the other side,
Don't let yourself turn a blind eye,
It is not necessary to fight back constantly.

There is a need to be impersonal every once in a while,
You need to learn to stop watering plants,
When they have already died.

SECTION 6:

I live so I love

In the hustle of daily life, I often find myself running short of words to say to the people I want to express my gratitude to.

This section is devoted to all the people, places, and things I love. 'I live so I love' serves as a reminder to all those without whose existence this book could never have become a reality. Love is a subjective feeling, and this section will also give a glimpse into my take on the question – 'What is love?'

1

LOSE YOUR HEART TO YOURSELF

Love yourself, they all say,
But is it really that easy?

To overlook all your flaws
And embrace the strengths,
To ignore all your ugliness,
And praise all your beauty.

I say, it is,
Cause you are an artist,
And your heart is your masterpiece.

It's time for you to realize,
That you are a gift to humanity,
A gift that is a sight for sore eyes.

It's time for you to rise to your true spirits,
And pour self-love into your heart,
Because there's no one who can love you,
The way you can.

Love yourself because you live,
Love yourself because you survive,
Love yourself because there's no one else
Who'll love you more than yourself.

2

LIFELINES

The world looks all blurry,
With these tears that brim my eyes,
All I can see is the colour black,
There's too much darkness for a rainbow.

Someone jolts me to consciousness,
Into their safe arms,
Wipes my wet cheeks,
And whispers, "It was just a dream, I'm here."

My saviour,
Mother.

And there's another person,
Who guides me through it all,
Standing by my side like a rock,
Protecting me from the cruel world.

He doesn't express himself much,

But his smallest gestures speak a million words,

I hope he knows I look up to him a lot,

After all, I am his only daughter,

And he will always be my number one hero.

3

MI CASA

Just like the warm colour yellow,
Your existence makes every predicament mellow.

The tears I shed don't hurt as much,
Because you're always by my side, holding an umbrella,
An umbrella to protect me from the rain of tears.

Growing up with you will always be special,
One makes a mistake, the other learns the double.

Even our bittersweet memories,
Are to me, beyond compare.

Sometimes, I fear losing you,
But then I find you smiling at me, so sweetly,
Exuding love and utter comfort,
Reminding me that you will always be my home.

A place where even silence feels warm,
And more importantly,
A place where I never feel alone,
My forever home.

4

LITTLE IS ENOUGH

Sometimes, I hear people say,

"I'm not good with words,

But I have so much to say."

In this text-driven world,

Where no one has the time to stop and read every line with regard,

Perhaps a few words are just about right,

To tell them all you want,

Words from your heart, filled with love and light.

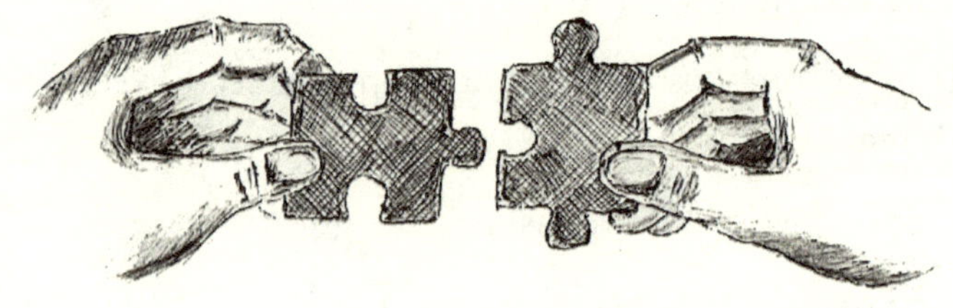

5

FOR YOU, MY FRIENDS

In a little world of my own,
Happen to exist these people,
Some I've known for years, and some for months.

I never really express my gratitude too openly,
Maybe, these words will change that.

No matter when you came into my life,
I hope you know, I learnt a lot from you.

Somewhere along the line,
You helped me become a better 'me'.

I cherish every smile and acknowledge every tear,
Every conversation has shaped my personality,
Every silence, cured my mind,
And everything in between, mattered to me.

Each one of you,
Gifted me with your existence,
In this little world of mine.

I hope you stay for long,
Hope you enjoy.

For now, all I can say is,
You are one of the many pieces,
That will help me put together,
The puzzle of my life.

6

'ONLINE FRIENDS'

We live miles apart,
But we talk like we're sitting right across,
What a delight it is,
To spend hours, talking our hearts out,
Making plans for our awaited rendezvous.

It seems like a fantasy,
To have someone know so much,
Without having crossed paths, not even once.

I certainly haven't said it enough,
Or might not have mentioned it ever,
But I'm glad I found a friend in you,
And now I can't wait,
For all that's to come my way.

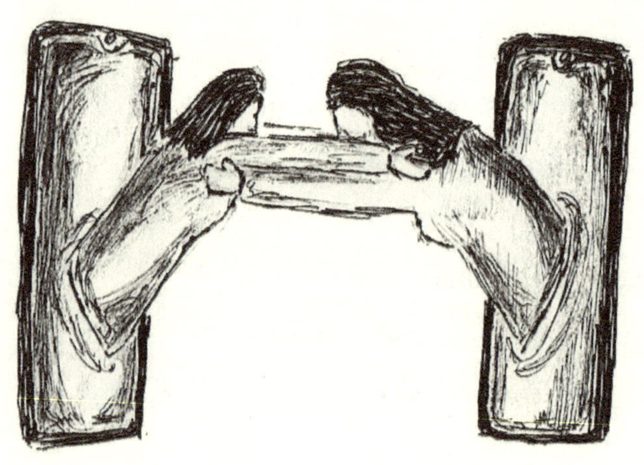

I'll make you experience it with me,

One day at a time,

Till we reach 'forever'.

7

LOVE

There are a million ways to describe love,
But limited ways to feel it.

The world says it knows love,
But does it truly?
One emotion that overcomes us all,
An illusion to many.

If you don't know what love is,
Don't fret,
Just thrust yourself into the beauty,
The beauty of it all.

Maybe, somewhere along the way,
You'll find a hidden treasure,
In something or someone,
And you'll feel a shift in the air,

With a content heart,
And a smile full of warmth.

With you, the love will get buried,
Into the depths,
Just to find a new owner someday,
And the legacy will pass on.

But till then,
Love is love.

A feeling often misinterpreted,
A word that is overused,
A hundred feelings muddled up into one,
A secret for the world.

8

FIRST LOVE

I may not have loved,
But I do have a lot to say,
First love isn't as magical,
As the whole world claims.

If your love wasn't bitter,
And all you tasted was sweetness,
Maybe, it wasn't love,
It was a sweet poison,
That kept feeding you with false hope,
Eating you up on the inside, little by little.

Why do people 'fall' in love?
When you can fly,
Into the endless blue sky,
And make love as beautiful as you say it feels.

And lastly, first love

Is a promise that you can't keep forever,

Because there are many more good things waiting for you.

You just need to open your eyes and wait,

And not use the word 'love' in vain.

9

SAFE AND SOUND

People think they're replaceable,
But in reality, they're not.

I returned from college a few weeks back,
And can state innumerable things that remind me
Of the people I shared my time with.

If you think you're forgettable,
Let me tell you how you're not.

You're simply unaware of the times,
When your friend is out there smiling,
At the joke they remember you cracking.

Someone was reminded of you,
When they heard the song, you made them listen to.

Many people think of you on your birthday,
Even if they don't bother to send a wish.

Just this way,
Little spaces will always be yours,
In the lives of all the people you've known.

Whether you like it or not,
Your existence is treasured in ways,
A lot more than you know about.

SECTION 7:

Outro: Life goes on

This is last section of my book, so I wanted to dedicate it to my belief that taking things at your pace is very courageous. I want these poems to be a reminder of the fact that all of us are allowed to live our lives in our own way, at our own pace. And that there is so much more to life than just worrying about the time passing by. I also wanted to talk about some things that we forget to mention, but still matter in the long run.

I hope you never forget that life goes on, no matter how much time it takes you to figure everything out. I hope you always remember that you are very strong for continuing to try.

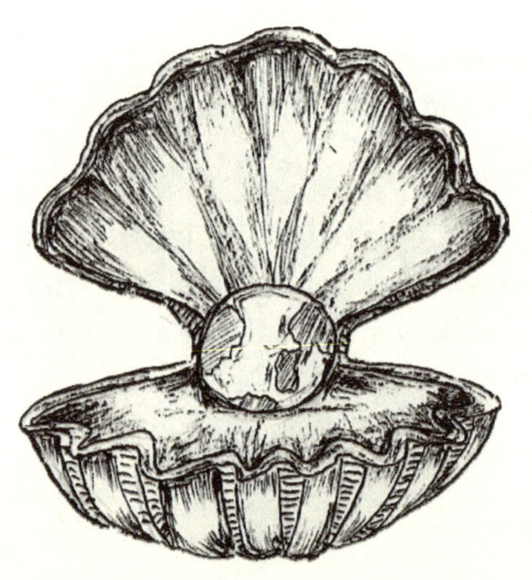

1

BEAUTY IN HUMANITY

Humans are unique, we are art,
There's just something too unreal about us all,
Ever since the day we are born,
We are different, yet we are not.

Notice how we learn the same letters,
But no handwriting is the same,
We all learn how to speak the same way,
Yet what we speak is such contrasting cadence.

We have almost similar bodies,
But what one can do, the other might not,
There's so many of us,
Floating around on this terrestrial planet,
Surrounded by utter nothingness.

Nevertheless,
What a relief that there are 7 billion of us,
What a relief that humans were born.

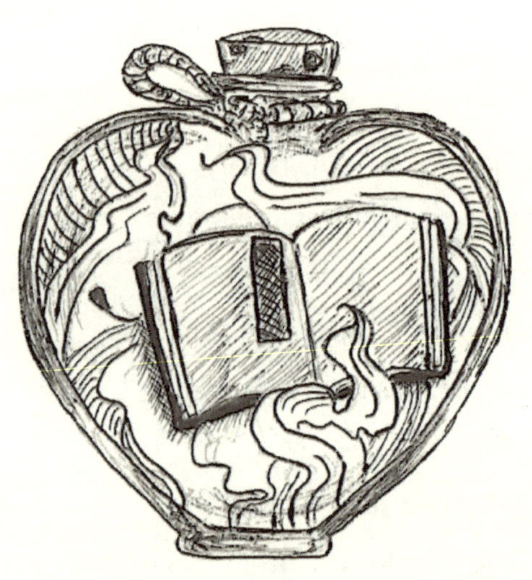

2

ABANDONED BUT NEVER LOST

We all grow out of habits we once had,
We all lose the love we once stored in the little hobbies,
That we nurtured with utmost care.

It's still such a pleasure to think of the times,
I started reading one book every week,
Till I was too weary to read any,
Or the time I was really into making jewellery,
Until I wasn't anymore.

Growing out of hobbies is natural,
Doesn't mean you're not skilled anymore,
Or have unlearned all that you mastered.

All hobbies you've ever had,
Are little bookmarks in the book of all your adventures,

No matter how insignificant,

Or how less time you spent with it.

It'll be labelled as a milestone,

Some little thrilling side-lines,

That pieced together your present form,

A learner, who learns from endeavours,

No matter how big or small.

3

SAVE A DYING FIRE

At times, when nothing feels right,
And the dark clouds start pouring from above,
Blowing out the fire inside of you,
Realize that maybe the 'you' you're looking for,
Grew into someone fully new.

The same person,
But with a different persona,
One who mutated because it was time,
To move ahead in a brand-new style.

So, instead of fighting constant battles
With yourself, inside your head,
Ignite your past self,
And give way to the one who was born,
From the 'you' who existed before, now fully gone.

It's okay if people change, totally fine if you did,
Change is natural,
Even if it is drastic.

Maybe, the person you knew,
Was a version you had created in your head,
A version that needed to be discarded.

4

STRENGTH IN SOFTNESS

One day, when I feel so burnt out,
That I sense flames spark in my soul,
And all I can utter,
Is a wish for a period of peace and quiet.

I hope that day,
My bones reduce to butterflies,
Taking away the all the pain.

It'll be the day
I pray the butterflies fly high,
Showing that there is strength in pausing.
You are courageous for stopping,
Before your body could set ablaze.

Time is just a ruthless construct,
That keeps running with no mercy,

It is not your duty to always stay at par,
With the seconds and minutes passing by.

Your duty is to keep yourself safe,
From the unforgiving pace of life,
There is bravery in willing to pause, to keep yourself alive.

5

POWER OF A SMILE

At every eye-contact I make,
I put a smile on my face,
In an attempt to wash away,
The worries of every stranger's life.

I know it might all go in vain,
But there is a reason why I don't give up.

We suffer every day,
While fighting our battles by ourselves,
Working endlessly when the sun's out,
Tossing and turning restlessly when the moon shines.

This is why I smile at people I don't even recognize,
Maybe, that one smile will be their reason to keep trying,
Perhaps, it will remind them,
That little joys weigh more that our hardships,

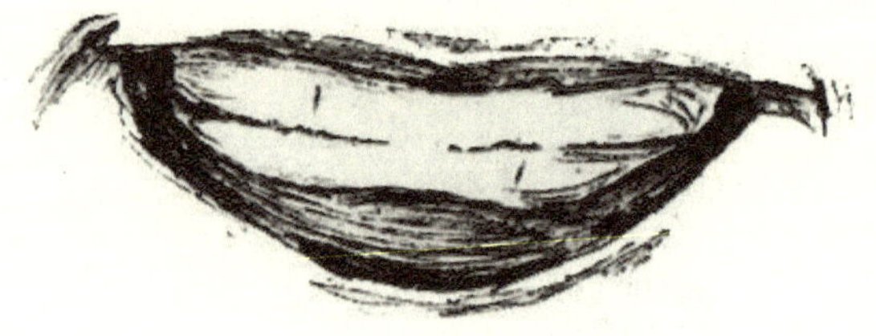

And that we're only human.

Creatures who smile,
To cancel out the pain,
A rebellion against every battle,
That disrupts the peace of our brain.

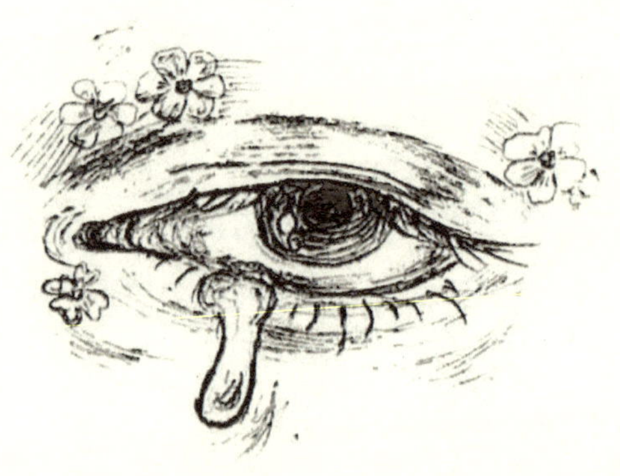

6

THOSE WHO CRY, FIGHT

Every tear is a lightning bolt,
Crashing through the surface of your eyes,
Making every colour seem less bright,
Bringing in a shower of sorrow,
One that doesn't feel too delightful.

A rain with a musty petrichor,
Where all the droplets mark a fissure,
A faint dent that keeps deepening,
Nullifying the sound of your heartbeat,
Tearing down all your insides.

Every cry you let out is a catastrophe,
That wrecks your stability,
And breaks you down,
Just like a star that exploded,
A supernova collapsing,
A beautiful facade now completely destroyed.

So, cave into the tears this once,
Let yourself fade a little,
So that when the clouds of despair dissipate,
The sunshine turns you bright,
All prepared for whatever is to come.

A victor of the war against tears,
The one who defeated the fierce storms of grief.

7

PERFECTION IS DEAD

In the fleeting moments of life,
I always wonder why everything has to be 'perfect'?
Why does every turn you take,
Have to end up at a predetermined destination?

Why do people stay up during the day,
And not during the night?

There's only one proper way to live life,
To be very honest,
Who even told us this lie?
There is freedom in doing things 'wrong',
Your world is an open playground,
It has been all along.

Go ahead and do everything your way,
Even if the whole world says, "That's not right",
Tell them it is your 'right'.

And if you're ever scared or worried,
Remember that pleasing people or their expectations,
Was never your responsibility.

You only live once,
And enjoying your life should your only priority.

www.ingramcontent.com/pod-product-compliance
Lightning Source LLC
La Vergne TN
LVHW091052150826
845673LV00002B/553